THE INTROVERT'S VIDEO MARKETING BLUEPRINT

6 Video Confidence Secrets

Bonus: Producer Checklist & Affordable Gear Guide Inside

AMANI CHANNEL

Copyright © 2019 by Amani Channel. All rights reserved.

No part of this publication may be reproduced, stored in a retrieval system or transmitted in any way by any means, electronic, mechanical, photocopy, recording or otherwise without the prior permission of the author except as provided by USA copyright law.

"You always have two choices:
Your commitment versus your fear."
~ Sammy Davis Jr.

THE TRUTH ABOUT VIDEO AND INTROVERTS

Is **being an introvert stopping you** from making videos?

If you think your personality is the problem...

This Might Turn Your World Upside Down

Some of the biggest YouTubers, celebrities, news personalities, and actors are introverted!

Do you know what **Grant Cardone**, **Warren Buffett**, **Hillary Clinton**, **Michael Jordan**, **Barack Obama**, and I (**Amani Channel**) have in common?

WE ARE INTROVERTS!

I don't see being an introvert as a negative thing.

Being **introverted is a gift**.

I'm **creative**.

I'm **non-confrontational**.

I'm fairly easy going and **easy to talk to**.

I **listen more than I speak**, so that means in some social situations, I'd rather be an observer than mingle it up.

Can you relate?

If you'd rather sit at home and **read a book** than chill out at a house party, you're probably an introvert.

If you're **super focused** (which I'm not); you're probably an introvert.

If you hate small talk but **enjoy thought-provoking conversations**, you're probably an introvert.

This is the thing...

A CAMERA CAN BE YOUR BEST FRIEND

The awesome thing about my method of speaking on camera is that **you will usually be all alone**, or with a small crew of people who want you to perform well on camera.

You will share a **short, helpful message** to one little inanimate device... a camera and hopefully, a microphone. Oops, that's two inanimate devices.

If you're **live,** it is broadcasted to a specific set of fans and followers and whatever you say or do will be seen by whoever is watching.

The other option is to **record a video**. I developed a simple method to remember and deliver your information on camera.

Once you've mastered my process for creating videos**, it will be so easy** that your current challenges won't even be a thought.

BONUS TIP: Don't worry about how you look or sound. It's more important to solve problems for your audience. *Confidence is an inside job.*

Andrea Varep Harrison
6 hrs

Dude, Amani thank you ... I lie low like all good introverts tend to but listen carefully and so appreciate your thoughts over the years - a little nothing video I posted organically to FB has 1,000 views - prior to you I would have pulled it down or changed the setting about 600 views ago - hahahaha - so thanks 🧡

 You, Andrea D. Smith and Kathleen Murray   1 Comment Seen by 3

How Do You Feel About Making Videos?

Is it **nerve-racking**?

When you record, do you feel **anxiety, fear**, or general **discomfort**?

Maybe you are **worried about saying something stupid** on camera, or you fear that saying the wrong thing will ruin your credibility and **people won't like you**.

A lot of people I help don't like how they **look or sound on camera**, especially at first.

Are you a **perfectionist** or **super self-critical**?

Do you worry about the **technical aspects** of making a video -- like what's the **best camera**, or **how to light**, and **where to shoot**?

These are all minor roadblocks in the way of your path to success.

AMANI CHANNEL

There is a ***science to discovering camera confidence***, and I developed a process that works, so keep reading because I'm going to share it in a moment.

 May Rabano shared a link to the group: Video Confidence Accelerator.
22 mins

Thanks to Amani, I'm proud to announce that I'm officially on YouTube. Omg, it has been a dream of mine to overcome anxiety when public speaking. Creating Videos is going to impact my business in a positive way. For those who wish to check out my progress from my first video here's a link to my YouTube Channel. I started with Non-speaking videos, then with Amani 's encouragement, I built up the courage to post speaking videos. It has been one hell of a journey, but THANK YOU from the bottom of my heart for helping me to overcome my fear. — 😁 feeling excited.

THE NUMBERS

If you don't understand why online video is a must, consider this:

- **Video is the number one** type of content that consumers want from brands.
- **6 out of 10 people** would rather **watch video online than TV**.
- **72%** of consumers want to **learn** about a new product or service (like yours) **via video**.
- And video is going to be **82% of all consumer internet traffic** in a few years.

But are you struggling to share even a simple message on camera?

I feel your pain.

I once had a huge problem sharing information on camera

If you're introverted (like me), camera shy, or just struggle with sharing a story on camera, this information will change all of that.

But this is the deal.

THIS WILL ONLY WORK IF YOU DO

I'm not talking about doing anything that will break a fingernail...

Or demand your first-born child.

All you have to do is **get out of your comfort zone** and **practice** making videos.

Just **get committed** to making videos and **listen** to some professional advice.

I've found that **coaches**, **course builders**, **service providers**, and mostly *fempreneurs and business owners* are my best students.

You can learn too.

MY FORMULA WORKS FOR ANYONE

- Introverts.
- Extroverts.
- Men or women.
- If you're looking for a video mentor.
- If you're ready to take action that can build your business, brand, or cause.
- If you're ready to add some automation into your business with videos, create a course, or attract prospects and leads.

Then, this might be right up your alley.

Like anything, **speaking on camera confidently** and making videos is all about **practice and reps**.

Just do things that build your video muscle, and you'll improve.

> Would you like to apply to a **FREE Camera Confidence Call**?
>
> https://www.videofearless.co/confidence-call
>
> If you have a pressing question or challenge, I have a few slots available for a limited time.

6 CAMERA CONFIDENCE SECRETS

I'm excited for you because I believe that if you're ready to take action, **you're closer than you think** to having a **video breakthrough**.

This is stuff that I normally charge for, so please don't take this lightly.

Please use this information to **conquer your fears** and **discover your confidence** because your influence can grow exponentially.

1 - COMMIT LIKE IT'S ALL ON THE LINE

The first step is **committing to video making and speaking on camera**. If you can make this a priority and habit, you will rapidly discover confidence.

Once you commit, **write down a start date** and learn as much as you can about video making. Join a video marketing Facebook group and don't be afraid to ask questions. You should commit to making videos at least once a week when you're starting, but two a week is even better.

> **ACTION ITEM:** I'm going to start making videos on _____.
>
> I'll continue to make videos weekly/monthly until I feel confident.

2 - GEAR UP LIKE A BOY SCOUT

To make videos, you'll need a **video camera** at a minimum and some accessories. I recommend you start with what you already have, like your **smartphone or webcam**.

This might surprise you. I'm a TV professional, but I like to keep my video marketing production set up simple and affordable.

If you have an existing video set up, disregard this information. But if you're starting at the ground floor, consider this basic gear for your home and mobile video productions.

Home Studio
1. Camera: Logitech c920 ($66)
2. Microphone: Audio Technica AT 2005 ($80)
3. Tripod (Optional): Joby ($75)
4. Light: Ring Light ($110)

Mobile Gear
1. Camera: Smartphone/Tablet
2. Microphone: RODE smartLav+ ($75) & extender cable ($25)
3. Tripod ($70) /Adaptor (Mobile Only) ($12)
4. Light: Ring Light ($110)

3 - PLAN LIKE A JEDI

This is probably the **most important step** in creating your video. How you plan for your video's success is paramount. **Plan it out** and **write it down.** You need to write down everything including the script, shoot location information, the date/time, overall video shots, any permissions like location and talent releases, and who is going to complete the edit. With video especially, failing to plan is planning to fail. Trust me. By the way, during this stage, you figure out what info you'll share with your audience, and create a general structure for your serial content. Here's an extra video jewel: Begin with the end in mind.

BONUS: Producer Checklist

Production Date & Time: Equipment:
Script: Edit:
Talent: Post Date:

I've developed a **framework to plan and message** your videos. We can discuss this during our 15-minute **Camera Confidence Call** https://www.videofearless.co/confidence-call.

4 - PRACTICE LIKE A PRO

Getting confident on camera is all about getting your reps in. That is how you'll start building your video muscle. **Practice as much as possible**. **Practice** in front of the bathroom mirror. **Practice** mentally. Practice on camera. You don't have to share it... But start recording on camera to get familiar with your equipment and always review your performance to figure out what could be done differently next time.

You probably won't like the way you sound at first. This is all I'm going to say, *Love Yourself*. Love your mannerisms and quirks. Your family members and clients love you, and your followers will too. But **only if you're being yourself on camera**. Don't copy or try to be someone else. People will connect to your authentic self - not a perfect caricature of what you think they want. If you're still really nervous, **practice more**. It should get easier to deliver your message each time you practice.

5 - RELAX AND FIND YOUR FLOW

I like to use the analogy of a musician to illustrate how important it is to **stay relaxed** during any kind of performance including recording a video. When you see world-class musicians playing, are they uptight or tense? No. They are in flow. They are one with the instrument and their hands, body, everything is relaxed. You will never perform well when you are tense or stressed out. If you're feeling anxious or nervous, the body is preparing for fight or flight instead of a flawless performance. This is why it's important to **relax your mind and body before you record.** Take some deep breaths, go to your happy place, or do a little yoga. Do whatever you need to get relaxed and comfortable. It is the most important skill to master when you're dealing with the pressure of performing on camera.

6 - PRESENT (RECORD/GO LIVE)

This is where the rubber hits the road. It's time to record. **Make sure the equipment is working**. Test your mic and check the shot and look for clutter or things that are out of place (this is important). Check the lighting. Make sure the audio is working and turn off the TV/music or anything that will distract the audience from your message.

If you're live, **be familiar with the live platform,** including how to start and stop the stream, and how to interact with your viewers and engage with them. Are you ready? Then review your talking points, take a deep breath or two, hit record or go live, and you're off.

The beauty of recording your message is that you can do it more than once, so don't get frustrated if you have to take multiple takes to get through your message. I suggest that you record a video that requires little to no editing, so **record your entire message in one take**. It might seem challenging at first, but you can do it. You're an expert and know the information like the back of your hand. If you are ready for the adventures of live, give it a shot. Just know that when you're live, you have to juggle a little bit more. There will be people to talk to, unexpected things will happen, it is a bit technical, and you have to hit your message points without much time to pause and think. But you can do it. I know you can because I do it, because my students are:

Misty Harris I met Amani Channel late last year and after talking to him, progressed quickly through his "Video Fearless" course. I have to say that his methods and guidance made me such a better online presenter than I could have imagined! I actually enjoyed and looked forward to doing live video.
He helped my business in so many ways because I refused to go on before taking his course because I didn't feel prepared or confident.
He is an expert in his field and his encouragement is helpful to get you moving along in the right direction.
Thanks, Amani!

Like · Reply · Message · 9w 2

VIDEO MARKETING

I believe that camera confidence is the foundation for all of your video marketing success.

That being said, I believe that learning how to **market with your videos is as important as becoming camera confident.**

A video marketing strategy will attract leads and customers, drive engagement, build relationships, and once that happens, life starts to get fun.

You can structure your business to get your time back.

You can spend more time with your family.

And you'll be in a better place to live life on your terms.

As you're working on your video marketing strategy, it's important to **develop a plan** that helps you reach a goal.

Make the goal **measurable** and set a **deadline**.

Then **measure** your results against your goal and adjust your strategy if needed.

Make sure you **know your audience** and know how to get your content in front of them.

Marketing is essential if you want to reap the benefits of video, but remember, you have to crawl before you walk…

No Confidence - No Credibility - No Authority

So, focus on your confidence, so that you'll be successful in your video marketing efforts.

WRAPPIN' UP

Now you know the **6 Secret Steps to Discover Your Confidence**.

1. Commit
2. Gear Up
3. Prepare
4. Practice
5. Relax
6. Record

GET STARTED

Please use this information now.

Like right now.

Hesitation breeds procrastination.

It's better to take baby steps than no steps at all.

And you must **be FearLESS**.

Before I conclude, I want to share a **story from one of my students.**

When I first decided to teach people how to become camera confident, I connected with a **law of attraction coach** named Charlotte Squire.

She wanted to make videos for an online course, but **she had a huge problem**.

Her **mind would always go blank** when it was time to go on camera.

During our initial Camera Confidence Call, I put her to the test and asked her a simple question.

Now, Charlotte lives in Germany and this call was via Zoom, but as soon as I asked the question, her demeanor changed.

She looked confused and couldn't answer the question.

After contemplating her predicament, I came up with a quick exercise.

Charlotte went along with it, and **by the end of the call, she was speaking on camera!**

After those quick results, **Charlotte enrolled** in my Video FearLESS **camera confidence program**, and the picture below speaks for itself!

 Charlotte Squire Your course, and your caring support has been a game-changer for me Amani, I never thought I would ever feel comfortable on video - and now it´s even really FUN and I get great feedback. THANKS! I highly recommended this opportunity to shine on video to any one else who is in the same position as I was: camera shy and a blank mind as soon as the camera started running. And it´s much more than that. It´s an allrounder with great tips and ressources.

Like · Reply · Message · 22w · Edited

If you're still reading this, you may be wondering if my solution will work for you?

Just **follow the six camera confidence secrets**, and please *reach out to me if you're ready for the fast track of video success*. Please use this link to schedule a time to talk https://www.videofearless.co/confidence-call.

What will your business and life look like if you started making awesome videos to market, connect with more people and build business relationships?

I'd love to help you with a specific plan to conquer your fear, discover your confidence to 5x your influence.

It's Time to Get Video FearLESS!!

Credits:

Page 3: Photo by Alexandru Zdrobău on Unsplash

Page 4: Photo by Andy Lee on Unsplash

Page 4: Photo by William Bayreuther on Unsplash

Page 8: Photo by Sam McGhee on Unsplash

ABOUT AMANI CHANNEL

Amani Channel, MA is an award-winning video producer and a former news reporter whose reports, content, and commentaries have been featured on NPR, CNN, Fox News Channel, HDNews, the Atlanta Journal Constitution, local news stations, and online outlets.

His early challenges as a news reporter with anxiety and camera fear led him to create Video FearLESS. He uses the system to help business owners conquer their fear, discover their confidence to 5x their influence. Or simply make kick ass videos.

Amani is a vlogging pioneer, and he's taught at the University of West Georgia, Kennesaw State University, and Hillsborough Community College. He's participated in workshops, conducted video training, and presented with Poynter Institute, the National Association of Black Journalists, Online News Association, Poynter Institute, Blog World (New Media Expo), and The Big Picture Conference.

AMANI CHANNEL

Contact: amani@videofearless.co
Website: www.videofearless.co
FB Group: Video Confidence Accelerator
IG: @amanichannel, @videofearless

www.ingramcontent.com/pod-product-compliance
Lightning Source LLC
Chambersburg PA
CBHW041211180526
45172CB00006B/1237